FASCISM

WHAT IT IS AND HOW TO FIGHT IT

LEON TROTSKY

SANAGE
PUBLISHING HOUSE

Copyright © 2020 Sanage Publishing House LLP

All rights reserved. No part of this publication may be reproduced, distributed, or transmitted in any form or by any means, including photocopying, recording, or other eletronic or mechanical methods, without the prior written permission of the publisher, except in the case of brief quotations embodied in critical reviews and certain other noncommercial uses permitted by copyright law. For permission requests, write to the publisher, addressed "Attention Permissions Coordinator," at the address below.

Paperback: 978-939574147-7

Any references to historical events, real people, or real places are used fictitiously. Names, characters, and places are products of the author's imagination.

Sanage Publishing House LLP
Mumbai, India

sanagepublishing@gmail.com

Lev Davidovich Bronstein (1879 – 1940), better known as **Leon Trotsky** was a Russian Marxist revolutionary, political theorist and politician. Ideologically a communist, he developed a variant of Marxism which has become known as Trotskyism.

Contents

1969 Pamphlet Introduction By George Lavan Weissman	5
Fascism – What Is It?	9
How Mussolini Triumphed	11
The Fascist Danger Looms In Germany	18
An Aesop Fable	24
The German Cops And Army	25
Bourgeoisie, Petty Bourgeoisie, And Proletariat	28
The Collapse Of Bourgeois Democracy	35
Does The Petty Bourgeoisie Fear Revolution?	38
The Workers' Militia And Its Opponents	41
The Perspective In The United States	53
BUILD THE REVOLUTIONARY PARTY!	56
Footnote by MIA	59

1969 PAMPHLET INTRODUCTION

By George Lavan Weissman

∽

Liberals and even most of those who consider themselves Marxists are guilty of using the world fascist very loosely today. They fling it around as an epithet or political swearword against right-wing figures whom they particularly despise, or against reactionaries in general.

Since WWII, the fascist label has been applied to such figures and movements as Gerald L.K. Smith, Senator Joseph McCarthy, Senator Eastland, Barry Goldwater, the Minutemen, the John Birch Society, Richard Nixon, Ronald Reagan, and George Wallace.

Now, were all these fascist, or just some? If only some, then how does one tell which are and which aren't?

Indiscriminate use of the term really reflects vagueness about its meaning. Asked to define fascism, the liberal replies in such terms as dictatorship, mass neurosis, anti-Semitism, the power of unscrupulous propaganda, the hypnotic effect of a mad-genius orator on the masses, etc. Impressionism and confusion on the part of liberals is not surprising. But Marxism's superiority consists of its ability to analyze and differentiate among social and political phenomena. that so many of those calling themselves marxists cannot define fascism any more adequately than the liberals is not wholly their fault. Whether they are aware of it or not, much of their intellectual heritage comes from the social-democratic (reformist socialist) and Stalinist movements, which dominated the left in the 1930s when fascism was scoring victory after victory. These movements not only permitted Nazism to come to power in Germany without a shot being fired against it, but they failed abysmally in understanding the nature and dynamics of fascism and the way to fight it. After fascism's triumphs, they had much to hide and so refrained from making a Marxist analysis which would, at least, have educated subsequent generations.

But there is a Marxist analysis of fascism. It was made by Leon Trotsky not as a postmortem, but during the rise of fascism. This was one of Trotsky's great contributions to Marxism. He began the task after Mussolini's victory in Italy in 1922 and brought it to a high point in the years preceding Hitler's triumph in Germany in 1933.

In his attempts to awaken the German Communist Party and the Communist International (Comintern) to the mortal danger and to rally a united-front against Nazism, Trotsky made a point-by-point critique of the policies of the social-democratic and Stalinist parties. This constitutes a compendium of almost all the mistaken, ineffective, and suicidal positions that workers' organizations can take regarding fascism, since the positions of the German parties ranged from opportunistic default and betrayal on the right (social democratic) to ultra-left abstentionism and betrayal (Stalinist).

The Communist movement was still on its ultra-left binge (the so-called Third Period) when the Nazi movement began to snowball. To the Stalinists, every capitalist party was automatically "fascist". Even more catastrophic than this disorienting of the workers was Stalin's famous dictum that, rather than being opposites, fascism and social democracy were "twins". The socialists were thereupon dubbed "social fascists" and regarded as the main enemy. Of course, there could be no united front with social-fascist organizations, and those who, like Trotsky, urged such united fronts, were also labeled social fascists and treated accordingly.

How divorced from reality the Stalinist line was may be illustrated be recalling its translation into American terms. In the 1932 elections, American Stalinists denounced Franklin Roosevelt as the fascist candidate and Norman Thomas as the social-fascist candidate. What was ludicrous as applied to US politics was tragic in Germany and Austria.

(Recently [1969], the term social fascism had begun cropping up in articles by members of the new left. Do those using it imagine that they have invented the term? Or, if they are aware of its history, are they indifferent to its connotations?)

After the Nazis came to power, the Stalinists boasted that their line had been 100 per cent correct, that Hitler could only last a few months, and that a Soviet Germany would then emerge. The time limit for this miracle was extended from three, six, to nine months, and then the idle boasts dwindled into silence. The magnitude of the defeat suffered by the working class, the special character of fascism, distinguishing it from other reactionary regimes or dictatorships, became apparent to all, and the threat to the Soviet Union or a rearmed German imperialism began to take on reality. This brought about a change in Moscow's line in 1935 and the Communist parties throughout the world thereupon zigzagged far to the right, to the right even of the social-democrats. This was their stance in the face of the spreading fascist danger in France and Spain.

The military ruin of German and Italian fascism in WWII convinced most people that fascism had been destroyed for good and was so utterly discredited that it could never again entice any followers.

Events since then, particularly the emergence of new fascist groups and tendencies in almost every capitalist country, have dispelled such wishful thinking. The illusion that WWII was fought to make the world safe from fascism has gone the way of the earlier illusion that WWI was fought to make the world safe for democracy. The germ of fascism is endemic in capitalism; a crisis can raise it to epidemic proportions unless drastic countermeasures are applied.

Since forewarned is forearmed, we offer this new compilation – a small selection from Trotsky's writings on the subject – as a weapon for the anti-fascist arsenal.

FASCISM – WHAT IS IT?

Extracts from a letter to an English comrade, November 15, 1931;
printed in **The Militant**, January 16, 1932

What is fascism? The name originated in Italy. Were all the forms of counter-revolutionary dictatorship fascist or not (That is to say, prior to the advent of fascism in Italy)?

The former dictatorship in Spain of Primo de Rivera, 1923–30, is called a fascist dictatorship by the Comintern. Is this correct or not? We believe that it is incorrect.

The fascist movement in Italy was a spontaneous movement of large masses, with new leaders from the rank and file. It is a plebian movement in origin, directed and financed by big capitalist powers. It issued forth from the petty bourgeoisie, the slum proletariat, and even to a certain extent from the proletarian masses; Mussolini, a former socialist, is a "self-made" man arising from this movement.

Primo de Rivera was an aristocrat. He occupied a high military and bureaucratic post and was chief governor of Catalonia. he accomplished his overthrow with the aid of state and military forces. The dictatorships of Spain and Italy are two totally different forms of dictatorship. It is necessary to distinguish between them. Mussolini had difficulty in reconciling many old military institutions with the fascist militia. This problem did not exist for Primo de Rivera.

The movement in Germany is analogous mostly to the Italian. It is a mass movement, with its leaders employing a great deal of socialist demagogy. This is necessary for the creation of the mass movement.

The genuine basis (for fascism) is the petty bourgeoisie. In italy, it has a very large base – the petty bourgeoisie of the towns and cities, and the peasantry. In Germany, likewise, there is a large base for fascism ...

It may be said, and this is true to a certain extent, that the new middle class, the functionaries of the state, the private administrators, etc., can constitute such a base. But this is a new question that must be analyzed ...

In order to be capable of foreseeing anything with regard to fascism, it is necessary to have a definition of that idea. What is fascism? What are its base, its form, and its characteristics? How will its development take place? It is necessary to proceed in a scientific and Marxian manner.

HOW MUSSOLINI TRIUMPHED

From **What Next? Vital Question for the German Proletariat**, 1932

At the moment that the "normal" police and military resources of the bourgeois dictatorship, together with their parliamentary screens, no longer suffice to hold society in a state of equilibrium – the turn of the fascist regime arrives. Through the fascist agency, capitalism sets in motion the masses of the crazed petty bourgeoisie and the bands of declassed and demoralized lumpenproletariat – all the countless human beings whom finance capital itself has brought to desperation and frenzy.

From fascism the bourgeoisie demands a thorough job; once it has resorted to methods of civil war, it insists on having peace for a period of years. And the fascist agency, by utilizing the petty bourgeoisie as a battering ram, by overwhelming all obstacles in its path, does a thorough job. After fascism is victorious, finance capital directly and immediately gathers into its hands, as in a vise of steel, all the organs and institutions of sovereignty, the executive administrative, and educational powers of the state: the entire state apparatus together with the army, the municipalities, the universities, the schools, the press, the trade unions, and the co-operatives. When a state turns fascist, it does not mean only that the forms and methods of government are changed in accordance the patterns set by Mussolini – the changes in this sphere ultimately play a minor role – but it means first of all for the most part that the workers' organizations are annihilated; that the proletariat is reduced to an amorphous state; and that a system of administration is created which penetrates deeply into the masses and which serves to frustrate the independent crystallization of the proletariat. Therein precisely is the gist of fascism ...

* * *

Italian fascism was the immediate outgrowth of the betrayal by the reformists of the uprising of the Italian proletariat. From the time the [first world] war ended, there was an upward trend in the revolutionary movement in Italy, and in September 1920 it resulted in the seizure of factories and industries by the workers. The dictatorship of the proletariat was an actual fact; all that was lacking was to organize it and draw from it all the necessary conclusions. The social democracy took fright and sprang back. After its bold and heroic exertions, the proletariat was left facing the void. The disruption of the revolutionary movement became the most important factor in the growth of fascism. In September, the revolutionary advance came to a standstill; and November already witnessed the first major demonstration of the fascists (the seizure of Bologna).

[NOTE: *The fascist campaign of violence began in Bologna, November 21, 1920. When the social-democratic councilmen, victorious in the municipal elections, emerged from city hall to present the new mayor, they were met by gunfire in which 10 were killed and 100 wounded. The fascists followed up with "punitive expeditions" into the surrounding countryside, a stronghold of the "Red Leagues". Blackshirt "action squadrons" in vehicles supplied by big landowners, took over villages in lightning raids, beating and killing leftist peasants and labor leaders, wrecking radical headquarters, and terrorizing the populace. Emboldened by their easy successes, the fascists then launched large-scale attacks in the big cities.]*

True, the proletariat, even after the September catastrophe, was capable of waging defensive battles. But the social democracy was concerned with only one thing: to withdraw the workers from combat at the cost of one concession after another. The social democracy hoped that the docile conduct of the workers would restore the "public opinion" of the bourgeoisie against the fascists. Moreover, the reformists even banked strongly upon the help of King Victor Emmanuel. To the last hour, they restrained the workers with might and main from giving battle to Mussolini's bands. It availed them nothing. The crown, along with the upper crust of the bourgeoisie, swung over to the side of fascism. Convinced at the last moment that fascism was not to be checked by obedience, the social democrats issued a call to the workers for a general strike. But their proclamation suffered a fiasco. The reformists had dampened the powder so long, in their fear lest it should explode, that when they finally with a trembling hand did apply a burning fuse to it, the powder did not catch.

Two years after its inception, fascism was in power. It entrenched itself thanks to the facts the first period of its overlordship coincided with a favorable economic conjuncture, which followed the depression of 1921–22. The fascists crushed the retreating proletariat by the onrushing forces of the petty bourgeoisie. But this was not achieved at a single blow. Even after he assumed power, Mussolini proceeded on his course with due caution: he lacked as yet ready-made models. During the first two years, not even the constitution was altered. The fascist government took on the character of a coalition. In the meantime, the fascist bands were busy at work with clubs, knives, and pistols. Only thus was the fascist government created slowly, which meant the complete strangulation of all independent mass organizations.

Mussolini attained this at the cost of bureaucratizing the fascist party itself. After utilizing the onrushing forces of the petty bourgeoisie, fascism strangled it within the vise of the bourgeois state. Mussolini could not have done otherwise, for the disillusionment of the masses he had united was precipitating itself into the most immediate danger ahead. Fascism, become bureaucratic, approaches very closely to other forms of military and police dictatorship. It no longer possesses its former social support. The chief reserve of fascism – the petty bourgeoisie – has been depicted. Only historical inertia enables the fascist government to keep the proletariat in a state of dispersion and helplessness....

In its politics as regards Hitler, the German social democracy has not been able to add a single word: all it does is repeat more ponderously whatever the Italian reformists in their own time performed with greater flights of temperament. The latter explained fascism as a postwar psychosis; the German social democracy sees in it a "Versailles" or crisis psychosis. In both instances, the reformists shut their eyes to the organic character of fascism as a mass movement growing out of the collapse of capitalism.

[NOTE: The Versailles Treaty, imposed on Germany after WWI; its most hated feature was the unending tribute to the victorious allies in the form of "reparations" for war damages and losses. The "crisis" referred to in the above paragraph was the economic depression that swept the capitalist world after the Wall Street crash of 1929.]

Fearful of the revolutionary mobilization of the workers, the Italian reformists banked all their hopes of the "state". Their slogan was, "Help! Victor Emmanuel, exert pressure!" The German social democracy lacks such a democratic bulwark as a monarch loyal to the constitution. So they must be content with a president – "Help! Hindenburg, exert pressure!"

[NOTE: Field Marshal Paul von Hindenburg (1847–1934), Junker

general who gained fame in World War I and later became president of the Weimar Republic. In 1932, the social democrats supported him for re-election as a "lesser evil" to the Nazis. He appointed Hitler chancellor in January 1933.]

While waging battle against Mussolini, that is, while retreating before him, Turati let loose his dazzling motto, "One must have the manhood to be a coward." [Filippo Turati (1857–1937), leading reformist theoretician of the Italian Socialist Party.] The German reformists are less frisky with their slogans. They demand "Courage under unpopularity" *(Mut zur Unpopularitaet)* – which amounts to the same thing. One must not be afraid of the unpopularity which has been aroused by one's own cowardly temporizing with the enemy.

Identical causes produce identical effects. Were the march of events dependent upon the social-democratic party leadership, Hitler's career would be assured.

One must admit, however, that the German Communist Party has also learned little from the Italian experience.

The Italian Communist Party came into being almost simultaneously with fascism. But the same conditions of revolutionary ebb tide, which carried the fascists to power, served to deter the development of the Communist Party. It did not give itself an accounting as to the full sweep of the fascist danger; it lulled itself with revolutionary illusions; it was irreconcilably antagonistic to the policy of the united front; in short, it was stricken with all the infantile diseases. Small wonder! It was only two years old. In its eyes, fascism appeared to be only "capitalist reaction". The *particular* traits of fascism which spring from the mobilization of the petty bourgeoisie against the proletariat, the Communist Party was unable to discern. Italian comrades inform me that, with the sole exception of Gramsci, the Communist Party would not even allow for the possibility of the fascists' seizing power. Once the proletarian revolution had suffered defeat, once capitalism had held its ground and the counter-revolution had triumphed, how could there be any further kind of counter-revolutionary upheaval? How could the bourgeoisie rise up against itself! Such was the gist of the political orientation of the Italian Communist Party. Moreover, one must not lose sight of the fact that Italian fascism was then a new phenomenon, just in the process of formation; it would not have been an easy task even for a more experienced party to distinguish its specific traits.

[NOTE: Antonio Gramsci (1891–1937): a founder of the Italian Communist Party, imprisoned by Mussolini in 1926, he died in prison 11 years later. He sent a letter from prison, in the name of the Italian party's political committee, protesting Stalin's campaign against the Left Opposition. Taglatti, then in Moscow as the Italian representative to the Comintern, suppressed the letter. Throughout the Stalin era, Gramsci's memory was deliberately effaced. In the period of de-Stalinization, however, he was "rediscovered" by the Italian Communist Party and officially enshrined as a hero and martyr. Since, there has been considerable international acclaim of his theoretical writings, particularly his prison notebooks.]

The leadership of the German Communist Party today reproduces almost literally the position from which the Italian Communists took their point of departure; fascism is nothing else but capitalist reaction; from the point of view of the proletariat, the difference between divers types of capitalist reaction are meaningless. This vulgar radicalism is the less excusable because the German party is much older than the Italian was at a corresponding period; in addition, Marxism is enriched now by the tragic experience in Italy. To insist that fascism is already here, or to deny the very possibility of its coming to power, amounts politically to one and the same thing. By ignoring the specific nature of of fascism, the will to fight against it inevitably becomes paralyzed.

The brunt of the blame must be borne, of course, by the

leadership of the Comintern. Italian Communists above all others were duty-bound to raise their voices in alarm. But Stalin, together with Manuilsky, compelled them to disavow the most important lessons of their own annihilation.

[NOTE: Dmitri Manuilsky (1883–1952): Headed the Comintern from 1929 to 1934; his removal heralded switch from ultra-leftism to the opportunism of the Popular Front period. Later appeared on diplomatic stage, as delegate to United Nations.]

We have already observed with what diligent alacrity Ercoli switched over to the position of social fascism – i.e., to the position of passively waiting for the fascist victory in Germany.

[NOTE: Ercoli. Comintern pen name of Palmiro Togliatti (1893–1964). Headed Italian Communist Party after Gramsci's imprisonment. He survived all zigzags in Comintern line, but after Stalin's death he criticized Stalin's rule as well some of its continuing features in the USSR and International Communist movement.]

THE FASCIST DANGER LOOMS IN GERMANY

From **The Turn in the Communist International and the German Situation**, 1930

The official press of the Comintern is now depicting the results of the [September 1930] German elections as a prodigious victory of Communism, which places on the order of the day the slogan of Soviet Germany. The bureaucratic optimists do not want to reflect upon the meaning of the relation of forces which is disclosed by the election statistics. They examine the figure of the increased Communist vote independently of the revolutionary tasks created by the situation and the obstacles it sets up. The Communist Party received around 4,600,000 votes as against 3,300,000 in 1928. From the viewpoint of "normal" parliamentary mechanics, the gain of 1,300,000 votes is considerable, even if we take into consideration the rise in the total number of voters. But the gain of the party pales completely beside the leap of fascism from 800,000 to 6,400,000 votes. Of no less important significance for evaluation the elections is the fact that the social democracy, in spite of substantial losses, retained its basic cadres and still received a considerably greater number of workers' votes [8,600,000] than the Communist Party.

Meanwhile, if we should ask ourselves, "What combination of international and domestic circumstances could be capable of turning the working class towards Communism with greater velocity?" we could not find an example of more favorable circumstances for such a turn than the situation in present-day Germany: Young's noose, the economic crisis, the disintegration of the rules, the crisis of parliamentarism, the terrific self-exposure of the social democracy in power. From the viewpoint of these concrete historical circumstances, the specific gravity of the German Communist Party in the social life of the country, in spite of the gain of 1,300,000 votes, remains proportionately small.

[NOTE: "Young's noose": a reference to the Young Plan. After Owen D. Young, American big businessman, who was Agent-General for the German Reparations during the 1920s. In summer of 1929, he was chairman of the conference which adopted his plan, which replaced the unsuccessful Dawes Plan, to "facilitate" Germany's payment of reparations as per the Treaty of Versailles.]

The weakness of the position of Communism, inextricably bound up with the policy and regime of the Comintern, is revealed more clearly if we compare the present social weight of the Communist Party with those concrete and unpostponable tasks which the present historical circumstances put before it.

It is true that the Communist Party itself did not expect such a gain. But this proves that under the blows of mistakes and defeats, the leadership of the Communist parties has become unused to big aims and perspectives. If yesterday it underestimated its own possibilities, then today it once more underestimates the difficulties. In this way, one danger is multiplied by another.

In the meantime, the first characteristic of a really revolutionary party is – to be able to look reality in the face.

* * *

In order that the social crisis may bring about the proletarian revolution, it is necessary that, besides other conditions, a decisive shift of the petty bourgeois classes occurs in the direction of the proletariat. This gives the proletariat a chance to put itself at the head of the nation as its leader.

The last election revealed – and this is where its principle symptomatic significance lies – a shift in the opposite direction. Under the blow of the crisis, the petty bourgeoisie swung, not in the direction of the proletarian revolution, but in the direction of the most extreme imperialist reaction, pulling behind it considerable sections of the proletariat.

The gigantic growth of National Socialism is an expression of two factors: a deep social crisis, throwing the petty bourgeois masses off balance, and the lack of a revolutionary party that would be regarded by the masses of the people as an acknowledged revolutionary leader. If the communist Party is the *party of revolutionary hope*, then fascism, as a mass movement, is the *party of counter-revolutionary despair*. When revolutionary hope embraces the whole proletarian mass, it inevitably pulls behind it on the road of revolution considerable and growing sections of the petty bourgeoisie. Precisely in this sphere the election revealed the opposite picture: counter-revolutionary despair embraced the petty bourgeois mass with such a force that it drew behind it many sections of the proletariat ...

Fascism in Germany has become a real danger, as an acute expression of the helpless position of the bourgeois regime, the conservative role of the social democracy in this regime, and the accumulated powerlessness of the Communist Party to abolish it. Whoever denies this is either blind or a braggart ...

The danger acquires particular acuteness in connection with the question of the *tempo* of development, which does not depend upon us alone. The malarial character of the political curve revealed by the election speaks for the fact that the tempo of development of the national crisis may turn out to be very speedy. In other words, the course of events in the very near future may resurrect in Germany, on a new historical plane, the old tragic contradiction between the maturity of a revolutionary situation, on the one hand, and the weakness and strategical impotence of the revolutionary party, on the other. This must be said clearly, openly and, above all, in time.

* * *

From Moscow, the signal has already been given for a policy of bureaucratic prestige which covers up the mistakes of yesterday and prepares tomorrow's by false cries about the new triumph of the line. Monstrously exaggerating the victory of the party, monstrously underestimating the difficulties, interpreting even the success of fascism as a positive factor for the proletarian revolution, Pravda nevertheless explains briefly: "The successes of the party should not make us dizzy." The treacherous policy of the Stalinist leadership is true to itself even here. The analysis of the situation is given in the spirit of uncritical ultraleftism. In this way the party is consciously pushed on the road of adventurism. At the same time, Stalin prepares his alibi in advance with the aid of the ritualistic phrase about "dizziness." It is precisely this policy, shortsighted, unscrupulous, that may ruin the German revolution. [A]

* * *

Can the strength of the conservative resistance of the social-democratic workers be calculated beforehand? It cannot. In the light of the events of the past year, this strength seems to be gigantic. But the truth is that what helped most of all to weld together social democracy was the wrong policy of the Communist Party, which found its highest generalization in the absurd theory of social fascism. To measure the real resistance of the social democratic ranks, a different measuring instrument is required, that is, a correct Communist tactic. With this condition – and it is not a small condition – the degree of internal unity of the social democracy can be revealed in a comparatively brief period.

In a different form, what has been said above also applies to fascism: It emanated, aside from the other conditions present, in the tremblings of the Zinoviev-Stalin strategy. What is its force for offensive? What is its stability? has it reached its culminating point, as the optimists ex-officio [Comintern and Communist Party officials] assure us, or is it only on the first step of the ladder? This cannot be foretold mechanically. It can be determined only through action. Precisely in regard to fascism, which is a razor in the hands of the class enemy, the wrong policy of the Comintern may produce fatal results in a brief period. On the other hand, a correct policy – not in such a short period, it is true – can undermine the positions of fascism ...

[NOTE: "Zinoviev-Stalin strategy": Gregory Y. Zinoviev (1883–1936), chairman of the Comintern from its founding in 1919 till his removal by Stalin in 1926. After Lenin's death, Zinoviev and Kamenev made a bloc with Stalin (the Troika) against Trotsky and dominated the Soviet party. In the period of the Zinoviev-Stalin domination of the Comintern, an opportunist line led to a series of defeats and missed opportunities, most notably the calling off of the German revolution of 1923. After breaking with Stalin, Zinoviev united his following with the Trotskyist Left Opposition. But in 1928, after the expulsion from the party of the United Opposition, Zinoviev capitulated to Stalin. Readmitted to the party, he was expelled again in 1932. After disavowal of all critical views, he was again readmitted, but in 1934, he was expelled and imprisoned. He "confessed" at the first of the great Moscow Trials in 1936 and was executed.]

If the Communist Party, in spite of the exceptionally favorable circumstances, has proved powerless seriously to shake the structure of the social democracy with the aid of the formula of "social fascism", then real fascism now threatens this structure, no longer with wordy formulae of so-called radicalism, but with the chemical formulas of explosives. No matter how true it is that the social democracy by its whole policy prepared the blossoming of fascism, it is no less true that fascism comes forward as a deadly threat primarily to that same social democracy, all of whose magnificence is inextricably bound with parliamentary-democratic-pacifist forms and methods of government …

The policy of a united front of the workers against fascism flows from this situation. It opens up tremendous possibilities to the Communist Party. A condition for success, however, is the rejection of the theory and practice of "social fascism", the harm of which becomes a positive measure under the present circumstances.

The social crisis will inevitably produce deep cleavages within the social democracy. The radicalization of the masses will affect the social democrats. We will inevitably have to make agreements with various social-democratic organizations and factions against fascism, putting definite conditions in this connection to the leaders, before the eyes of the masses … We must return from the empty official phrase about the united front to the policy of the united front as it was formulated by Lenin and always applied by the Bolsheviks in 1917.

AN AESOP FABLE

From **What Next? Vital Question for the German Proletariat**, 1932

A cattle dealer once drove some bulls to the slaughterhouse. And the butcher came nigh with his sharp knife.

"Let us close ranks and jack up this executioner on our horns," suggested one of the bulls.

"If you please, in what way is the butcher any worse than the dealer who drove us hither with his cudgel?" replied the bulls, who had received their political education in Manuilsky's institute. [The Comintern.]

"But we shall be able to attend to the dealer as well afterwards!"

"Nothing doing," replied the bulls firm in their principles, to the counselor. "You are trying, from the left, to shield our enemies – you are a social-butcher yourself."

And they refused to close ranks.

* * *

THE GERMAN COPS AND ARMY

From **What Next? Vital Question for the German Proletariat**, 1932

In case of actual danger, the social democracy banks not on the "Iron Front" but on the Prussian police. It is reckoning without its host! The fact that the police was originally recruited in large numbers from among social-democratic workers is absolutely meaningless. Consciousness is determined by environment even in this instance. The worker who becomes a policeman in the service of the capitalist state, is a bourgeois cop, not a worker. Of late years, these policemen have had to do much more fighting with revolutionary workers than with Nazi students. Such training does not fail to leave its effects. And above all: every policeman knows that though governments may change, the police remains.

[NOTE: "The Iron Front": A bloc between several big trade unions and bourgeois "republican" groups with little or no following or prestige among the masses. It was created by the social democrats toward the end of 1931. Combat groups called the Iron Fist were set up within the unions, and workers' sports organizations were brought into the Iron Front. However, its first parades and rallies, at which

thousands of workers raised their fists, shouted "Freedom", and swore to defend democracy. The masses in the Social Democratic Party and unions really believed that this organization would be used to stop Hitler. It was not.]

In its New Year's issue, the theoretical organ of the social democracy, *Dar Freie Wort* (what a wretched sheet!), prints an article in which the policy of "toleration" is expounded in its highest sense. Hitler, it appears, can never come to power against the police and the Reichswehr [German army]. Now, according to the constitution, the Reichswehr is under the command of the president of the Republic. Therefore fascism, it follows, is not dangerous so long as a president faithful to the constitution remains at the head of the government. Bruening's regime must be supported until the presidential elections so that a constitutional president may then be elected, through an alliance with the parliamentary bourgeoisie; and thereby Hitler's road to power will be blocked for another seven years ...

[NOTE: Heinrich Bruening was chancellor from 1930–32. Regular parliamentary government in Germany ended in March 1930. There followed a series of Bonapartist regimes – Bruening, von Papen, von Schleicher, i.e., chancellors ruling not by ordinary parliamentary procedures but by "emergency" decrees. These Bonapartist figures presented themselves as political saviors needed to get the country through its crisis, and thus as above class and party. They depended not on the old bourgeois democratic party system but on their command of the police, army, and government bureaucracy. Pretending to be saving the nation from the dangers on both the left (socialists and communists) and the right (fascists), they struck their heaviest blows against the left, since their primary interest was saving capitalism.]

The politicians of reformism, these dexterous wire-pullers, artful intriguers and careerists, expert parliamentary and ministerial machinators, are no sooner thrown out of their habitual sphere by the course of events, no sooner are the placed face to face with momentous contingencies than they reveal themselves to be – there is no milder expression for it – inept bodies.

To rely upon a president is only to rely upon "the government"! Faced with the impending clash between the proletariat and the fascist petty bourgeoisie – two camps which together comprise the crushing majority of the German nation – these Marxists from the Vorwaerts [principal social-democratic newspaper] yelp for the nightwatchman to come to their aid, "Help! Government, exert pressure!" (*Staat, greif zu!*)

BOURGEOISIE, PETTY BOURGEOISIE, AND PROLETARIAT

From **The Only Road for Germany** written September 1932, published in the USA April 1933

Any serious analysis of the political situation must take as its point of departure the mutual relations among the three classes: the bourgeoisie, the petty bourgeoisie (including the peasantry), and the proletariat.

The economically powerful big bourgeoisie, in itself, represents an infintesimal minority of the nation. To enforce its domination, it must ensure a definite mutual relationship with the petty bourgeoisie and, through its mediation, with the proletariat.

To understand the dialectic of the relation among the three classes, we must differentiate three historical stages: at the dawn of capitalistic development, when the bourgeoisie required revolutionary methods to solve its tasks; in the period of bloom and maturity of the capitalist regime, when the bourgeoisie endowed its domination with orderly, pacific, conservative, democratic forms; finally, at the decline of capitalism, when the bourgeoisie is forced to resort to methods of civil war against proletariat to protect its right of exploitation.

The political programs characteristic of these three stages – JACOBINISM [left wing of petty bourgeois forces in Great French Revolution; in most revolutionary phase, led by Robespierre], reformist DEMOCRACY (social democracy included), and FASCISM – are basically programs of petty bourgeois currents. This fact alone, more than anything else, shows of what tremendous – rather, of what decisive – importance the self-determination of the petty bourgeois masses of the people is for the whole fate of bourgeois society.

Nevertheless, the relationship between the bourgeoisie and its basic social support, the petty bourgeoisie, does not at all rest upon reciprocal confidence and pacific collaboration. In its mass, the petty bourgeoisie is an exploited and disenfranchised class. It regards the bourgeoisie with envy and often with hatred. The bourgeoisie, on the other hand, while utilizing the support of the petty bourgeoisie, distrusts the latter, for it very correctly fears its tendency to break down the barriers set up for it from above.

While they were laying out and clearing the road for bourgeois development, the Jacobins engaged, at every step, in sharp clashes with the bourgeoisie. They served it in intransigent struggle against it. After they had culminated their limited historical role, the Jacobins fell, for the domination of capital was predetermined.

For a whole series of stages, the bourgeoisie entrenched its power under the form of parliamentary democracy. Even then, not peacefully and not voluntarily. The bourgeoisie was mortally afraid of universal suffrage. But in the last instance, it succeeded, with the aid of a combination of violent measures and concessions, of privations and reforms, in subordinating within the framework of formal democracy not only the petty bourgeoisie but in considerable measure also the proletariat, by means of the new petty bourgeoisie – the labor aristocracy. In August 1914, the imperialist bourgeoisie was able, with the means of parliamentary democracy, to lead millions of workers and peasants into the war.

[NOTE: August 4, 1914: collapse of the Second International. The German Social-Democratic Party representatives in the Reichstag voted for the war budget of the imperialist governments; on the same day, representatives of the French Socialist Party did likewise in the Chamber of Deputies.]

But precisely with the war begins the distinct decline of capitalism and, above all, of its democratic form of domination. It is now no longer a matter of new reforms and alms, but of cutting down and abolishing the old ones. Therewith the bourgeoisie comes into conflict into only with the institutions of proletarian democracy (trade unions and political parties) but also with parliamentary democracy, within the framework of which arose the labor organizations. Therefore, the campaign against "Marxism" on the one hand and against democratic parliamentarism on the other.

But just as the summits of the liberal bourgeoisie in its time were unable, by their own force alone, to get rid of feudalism, monarchy, and the church, so the magnates of finance capital are unable, by their force alone, to cope with the proletariat. They need the support of the petty bourgeoisie. For this purpose, it must be whipped up, put on its feet, mobilized, armed. But this method has its dangers. While it makes use of fascism, the bourgeoisie nevertheless fears it. Pilsudski was forced, in May 1926, to save bourgeois society by a coup d'etat directed against the traditional parties of the Polish bourgeoisie. The matter went so far that the official leader of the Polish Communist Party, Warski, who came over from Rosa Luxemburg not to Lenin but to Stalin, took the coup d'etat of Pilsudski to be the road of the "revolutionary democratic dictatorship" and called upon the workers to support Pilsudski.

[NOTE: Joseph Pilsudski (1876–1935): Originally a socialist with nationalistic views, in 1920 he led the anti-Soviet forces in Poland; in 1926, he led a coup d'etat and established a fascist dictatorship. Warski: Friend of Rosa Luxemburg, he supported her differences with the Bolsheviks. When Comintern zigzagged to the left in its "Third Period" phase, Warski was demoted from leadership in the Polish Communist Party, but not expelled. He disappeared in the USSR during the great purge of 1936–38. Rosa Luxemburg (1870–1919): Great revolutionary theoretician and leader. Originally active in socialist movement of her native Poland, she later became a leader of the left wing of the German Social-Democratic Party. She and Karl Liebknecht were imprisoned for opposing World War I. After their release, they led the Spartakusbund. Both were arrested and assassinated during the unsuccessful revolution of 1919.]

At the session of the Polish Commission of the Executive Committee of the Communist International on July 2, 1926, the author of these lines said on the subject of the events in Poland:

"Taken as a whole, the Pilsudski overthrow is the petty bourgeois, 'plebian' manner of solving the burning problems of bourgeois society in its state of decomposition and decline. We have here already a direct resemblance to Italian fascism.

"These two currents indubitably possess common features: they recruit their shock troops first of all from the petty bourgeoisie; Pilsudski as well as Mussolini worked with extra-parliamentary means, with open violence, with the methods of civil war; both were concerned not with the destruction but with the preservation of bourgeois society. While they raised the petty bourgeoisie on its feet, they openly aligned themselves, after the seizure of power, with the big bourgeoisie. Involuntarily, a historical generalization comes up here, recalling the evaluation given by Marx of Jacobinism as the plebian method of settling accounts with the feudal enemies of the bourgeoisie ... That was in the period of the rise of the bourgeoisie. Now we must say, in the period of the decline of bourgeois society, the bourgeoisie again needs the 'plebian' method of resolving its no longer progressive but entirely reactionary tasks. In this sense, fascism is a caricature of Jacobinism.

"The bourgeoisie is incapable of maintaining itself in power by the means and methods of the parliamentary state created by itself; it needs fascism as a weapon of self-defense, at least in critical instances. Nevertheless, the bourgeoisie does not like the 'plebian' method of resolving its tasks. It was always hostile of Jacobinism, which cleared the road for the development of bourgeois society with its blood. The fascists are immeasurably closer to the decadent bourgeoisie than the Jacobins were to the rising bourgeoisie. Nevertheless, the sober bourgeoisie does not look very favorably even upon the fascist mode of resolving its tasks, for the concussions, although they are brought forth in the interests of bourgeois society, are linked up with dangers to it. Therefore, the opposition between fascism and the bourgeois parties.

"The big bourgeoisie likes fascism as little as a man with aching molars likes to have his teeth pulled. The sober circles of bourgeois society have followed with misgivings the work of the dentist Pilsudski, but in the last analysis they have become reconciled to the inevitable, though with threats, with horse-trades and all sorts of bargaining. Thus the petty bourgeoisie's idol of yesterday becomes transformed into the gendarme of capital."

To this attempt at marking out the historical place of fascism as the political reliever of the social democracy, there was counterposed the theory of social fascism. At first it could appear as a pretentious, blustering, but harmless stupidity. Subsequent events have shown what a pernicious influence the Stalinist theory actually exercised on the entire development of the Communist

International.

Does it follow from the historical role of Jacobinism, of democracy, and of fascism, that the petty bourgeoisie is condemned to remain a tool in the hands of capital to the end of its days? It things were so, then the dictatorship of the proletariat would be impossible in a number of countries in which the petty bourgeoisie constitutes the majority of the nation and, more than that, it would be rendered extremely difficult in other countries in which the petty bourgeoisie represents an important minority. Fortunately, things are not so. The experience of the Paris Commune [first "dictatorship of the proletariat", March 18, 1871] first showed, at least within the limits of one city, just as the experience of the October Revolution [Russian Revolution of 1917] has shown after it on a much larger scale and over an incomparably longer period, that the alliance of the petty bourgeoisie and the big bourgeoisie is not indissoluble. Since the petty bourgeoisie is incapable of an independent policy (that is also why the petty bourgeois "democratic dictatorship" is unrealizable), no other choice is left for it than that between the bourgeoisie and the proletariat.

In the epoch of the rise, the growth, and the bloom of capitalism, the petty bourgeoisie, despite acute outbreaks of discontent, generally marched obediently in the capitalist harness. Nor could it do anything else. But under the conditions of capitalist disintegration, and of the impasse in the economic situation, the petty bourgeoisie strives, seeks, attempts to tear itself loose from the fetters of the old masters and rulers of society. It is quite capable of linking up its fates with that of the proletariat. For that, only one thing is needed: the petty bourgeoisie must acquired faith in the ability of the proletariat to lead society onto a new road. The proletariat can inspire this faith only by its strength, by the firmness of its actions, by a skillful offensive against the enemy, by the success of its revolutionary policy.

But, woe, if the revolutionary party does not measure up to

the height of the situation! The daily struggle of the proletariat sharpens the instability of bourgeois society. The strikes and the political disturbances aggravated the economic situation of the country. The petty bourgeoisie could reconcile itself temporarily to the growing privations, if it arrived by experience at the conviction that the proletariat is in a position to lead it onto a new road. But if the revolutionary party, in spite of a class struggle becoming incessantly more accentuated, proves time and again to be incapable of uniting the working class about it, if it vacillates, becomes confused, contradicts itself, then the petty bourgeoisie loses patience and begins to look upon the revolutionary workers as those responsible for its own misery. All the bourgeois parties, including the social democracy, turn its thoughts in this very direction. When the social crisis takes on an intolerable acuteness, a particular party appears on the scene with the direct aim of agitating the petty bourgeoisie to a white heat and of directing its hatred and its despair against the proletariat. In Germany, this historical function is fulfilled by national Socialism (Nazism), a broad current whose ideology is composed of all the putrid vapors of disintegrating bourgeois society.

THE COLLAPSE OF BOURGEOIS DEMOCRACY

From **Whither France?**, 1934

After the war, a series of brilliantly victorious revolutions occurred in Russia, Germany, Austria-Hungary, and later in Spain. But it was only in Russia that the proletariat took full power into its hands, expropriated its exploiters, and knew how to create and maintain a workers' state. Everywhere else the proletariat, despite its victory, stopped halfway because of the mistakes of its leadership. As a result, power slipped from its hands, shifted from left to right, and fell prey to fascism. In a series of other countries, power passed into the hands of a military dictatorship. Nowhere were the parliaments capable of reconciling class contradictions and assuring the peaceful development of events. Conflicts were solved arms in hand.

The French people for a long time thought that fascism had nothing whatever to do with them. They had a republic in which all questions were dealt with by the sovereign people through the exercise of universal suffrage. But on February 6, 1934, several thousand fascists and royalists, armed with revolvers, clubs, and razors, imposed upon the country the reactionary government of Doumergue, under whose protection the fascist bands continue to grow and arm themselves. What does tomorrow hold?

[NOTE: Gaston Doumergue: Bonapartist premier of France. Succeeded Edouard Daladier. Daladier government fell the day after the fascist riots of February 6, 1934.]

Of course, in France, as in certain other European countries (England, Belgium, Holland, Switzerland, the Scandinavian countries), there still exist parliaments, elections, democratic liberties, or their remnants. But in all these countries, the same historic laws operate, the laws of capitalist decline. If the means of production remain in the hands of a small number of capitalists, there is no way out for society. It is condemned to go from crisis to crisis, from need to misery, from bad to worse. In the various countries, the decrepitude and disintegration of capitalism are expressed in diverse forms and at unequal rhythms. But the basic features of the process are the same everywhere. The bourgeoisie is leading its society to complete bankruptcy. It is capable of assuring the people neither bread nor peace. This is precisely why it cannot any longer tolerate the democratic order. It is forced to smash the workers and peasants by the use of physical violence. The discontent of the workers and peasants, however, cannot be brought to an end by the police alone. Moreover, if it often impossible to make the army march against the people. It begins by disintegrating and ends with the passage of a large section of the soldiers over to the people's side. That is why finance capital is obliged to create special armed bands, trained to fight the workers just as certain breeds of dog are trained to hunt game. The historic function of fascism is to smash the working class, destroy its organizations, and stifle political liberties when the capitalists find themselves unable to govern and dominate with the help of democratic machinery.

The fascists find their human material mainly in the petty

bourgeoisie. The latter has been entirely ruined by big capital. There is no way out for it in the present social order, but it knows of no other. Its dissatisfaction, indignation, and despair are diverted by the fascists away from big capital and against the workers. It may be said that fascism is the act of placing the petty bourgeoisie at the disposal of its most bitter enemies. In this way, big capital ruins the middle classes and then, with the help of hired fascist demagogues, incites the despairing petty bourgeoisie against the worker. The bourgeois regime can be preserved only by such murderous means as these. For how long? Until it is overthrown by proletarian revolution.

DOES THE PETTY BOURGEOISIE FEAR REVOLUTION?

From **Whither France?**, 1934

Parliamentary cretins, who consider themselves connoisseurs of the people, like to repeat:

"One must not frighten the middle classes with revolution. They do not like extremes."

In this general form, this affirmation is absolutely false. Naturally, the petty proprietor prefers order so long as business is going well and so long as he hopes that tomorrow it will go better.

But when this hope is lost, he is easily enraged and is ready to give himself over to the most extreme measures. Otherwise, how could he have overthrown the democratic state and brought fascism to power in Italy and Germany? The despairing petty bourgeois sees in fascism, above all, a fighting force against big capital, and believes that, unlike the working-class parties which deal only in words, fascism will use force to establish more "justice". The peasant and the artisan are in their manner realists. They understand that one cannot forego the use of force.

It is false, thrice false, to affirm that the present petty bourgeoisie is not going to the working-class parties because it fears "extreme measures". Quite the contrary. The lower petty bourgeoisie, its great masses, only see in the working-class parties parliamentary machines. They do not believe in their strength, nor in their capacity to struggle, nor in their readiness this time to conduct the struggle to the end.

And if this is so, is it worth the trouble to replace the democratic capitalist representatives by their parliamentary confreres on the left? That is how the semi-exploited, ruined, and discontented proprietor reasons of feels. Without an understanding of this psychology of the peasants, the artisans, the employees, the petty functionaries, etc. – a psychology which flows from the social crisis – it is impossible to elaborate a correct policy. The petty bourgeoisie is economically dependent and politically atomized. That is why it cannot conduct an independent policy. It needs a "leader" who inspires it with confidence. This individual or collective leadership, i.e., a personage or party, can be given to it by one or the other of the fundamental classes – either the big bourgeoisie or the proletariat. Fascism unties and arms the scattered masses. Out of human dust, it organizes combat detachments. It thus gives the petty bourgeoisie the illusion of being an independent force. It begins to imagine that it will really command the state. It is not surprising that these illusions and hopes turn the head of the petty bourgeoisie!

But the petty bourgeoisie can also find a leader in the proletariat. This was demonstrated in Russia and partially in Spain. In Italy, in Germany, and in Austria, the petty bourgeoisie gravitated in this direction. But the parties of the proletariat did not rise to their historic task.

To bring the petty bourgeoisie to its side, the proletariat must win its confidence. And for that it must have confidence in its own strength.

It must have a clear program of action and must be ready to struggle for power by all possible means. Tempered by it revolutionary party for a decisive and pitiless struggle, the proletariat says to the peasants and petty bourgeoisie of the cities:

> "We are struggling for power. Here is our program. We are ready to discuss with you changes in this program. We will employ violence only against big capital and its lackeys, but with you toilers, we desire to conclude an alliance on the basis of a given program."

The peasants will understand such language. Only, they must have faith in the capacity of the proletariat to seize power.

But for that it is necessary to purge the united front of all equivocation, of all indecision, of all hollow phrases. It is necessary to understand the situation and to place oneself seriously on the revolutionary road.

THE WORKERS' MILITIA AND ITS OPPONENTS

From **Whither France?**, 1934

To struggle, it is necessary to conserve and strengthen the instrument and the means of struggle – organizations, the press, meetings, etc. Fascism [in France] threatens all of that directly and immediately. It is still too weak for the direct struggle for power, but it is strong enough to attempt to beat down the working-class organizations bit by bit, to temper its bands in its attacks, and to spread dismay and lack of confidence in their forces in the ranks of the workers.

Fascism finds unconscious helpers in all those who say that the "physical struggle" is impermissible or hopeless, and demand of Doumergue the disarmament of his fascist guard. Nothing is so dangerous for the proletariat, especially in the present situation, as the sugared poison of false hopes. Nothing increases the insolence of the fascists so much as "flabby pacificism" on the part of the workers' organizations. Nothing so destroys the confidence of the middle classes in the working-class as temporizing, passivity, and the absence of the will to struggle.

Le Populaire [the Socialist Party paper] and especially **l'Humanité** [the Communist Party newspaper] write every day:

> "The united front is a barrier against fascism"; "the united front will not permit ..."; "the fascists will not dare", etc.

These are phrases. It is necessary to say squarely to the workers, Socialists, and Communists: do not allow yourselves to be lulled by the phrases of superficial and irresponsible journalists and orators. It is a question of our heads and the future of socialism. It is not that we deny the importance of the united front. We demanded it when the leaders of both parties were against it. The united front opens up numerous possibilities, but nothing more. In itself, the untied front decides nothing. Only the struggle of the masses decides. The untied front will reveal its value when Communist detachments will come to the help of Socialist detachments nd vice versa in the case of an attack by the fascist bands against **Le Populaire** or **l'Humanité**. But for that, proletarian combat detachments must exist and be educated, trained, and armed. And if there is not an organization of defense, i.e., a workers' militia, **Le Populaire** or **l'Humanité** will be able to write as many articles as they like on the omnipotence of the united front, but the two papers will find themselves defenseless before the first well-prepared attack of the fascists.

We propose to make a critical study of the "arguments" and the "theories" of the opponents of the workers' militia who are very numerous and influential in the two working-class parties.

> "We need mass self-defense and not the militia," we are often told.

But what is this "mass self-defense" without combat organizations, without specialized cadres, without arms? To give over the defense against fascism to unorganized and unprepared masses left to themselves would be to play a role incomparably lower than the role of Pontius Pilate. To deny the role of the militia is to deny the role of the vanguard. Then why a party? Without the support of the masses, the militia is nothing. But without organized combat detachments, the most heroic masses will be smashed bit by bit by the fascist gangs. It is nonsense to counterpose the militia to self-defense. The militia is an organ of self-defense.

> "To call for the organization of a militia," say some opponents who, to be sure, are the least serious and honest, "is to engage in provocation."

This is not an argument but an insult. If the necessity for the defense of the workers' organizations flows from the whole situation, how then can one not call for the creation of the militia? Perhaps they mean to say that the creation of a militia "provokes" fascist attacks and government repression. In that case, this is an absolutely reactionary argument. Liberalism has always said to the workers that by their class struggle they "provoke" the reaction.

The reformists repeated this accusation against the Marxists, the Mensheviks against the Bolsheviks. These accusations reduced themselves, in the final analysis, to the profound thought that if the oppressed do not balk, the oppressors will not be obliged to beat them. This is the philosophy of Tolstoy and Gandhi but never that of Marx and Lenin. If l'**Humanité** wants hereafter to develop the doctrine of "non-resistance to evil by violence", it should take for its symbol not the hammer and sickle, emblem of the October Revolution, but the pious goat, which provides Gandhi with his milk.

> "But the arming of the workers is only opportune in a revolutionary situation, which does not yet exist."

This profound argument means that the workers must permit themselves to be slaughtered until the situation becomes revolutionary. Those who yesterday preached the "third period" do not want to see what is going on before their eyes. The question of arms itself has come forward only because the "peaceful", "normal", "democratic" situation has given way to a stormy, critical, and unstable situation which can transform itself into a revolutionary, as well as a counter-revolutionary, situation.

[NOTE: "The Third Period": According to the Stalinist schema, this was the "final period of capitalism", the period of its immediately impending demise and replacement by soviets. The period is notable for the Communists' ultra-left and adventurist tactics, notably the concept of social-fascism.]

This alternative depends above all on whether the advanced workers will allow themselves to be attacked with impunity and defeated bit by bit or will reply to every blow by two of their own, arousing the courage of the oppressed and uniting them around their banner. A revolutionary situation does not fall from the skies. It takes form with the active participation of the revolutionary class and its party.

The French Stalinists now argue that the militia did not safeguard the German proletariat from defeat. Only yesterday they completely denied any defeat in Germany and asserted that the policy of the German Stalinists was correct from beginning to end. Today, they see the entire evil in the German workers' militia (*Rote Front*) [i.e., Red Front Fighters: Communist-dominated militia banned by the social-democratic government after the Berlin May Day riots of 1929]. Thus, from one error they fall into a diametrically opposite one, no less monstrous. The militia, in itself, does not settle the question. *A correct policy is necessary.* Meanwhile, the policy of Stalinism in Germany ("social fascism is the chief enemy"), the split in the trade unions, the flirtation with nationalism, putschism) fatally led to the isolation of the proletarian vanguard and to its shipwreck. With an utterly worthless strategy, no militia could have saved the situation.

It is nonsense to say that, in itself, the organization of the militia leads to adventures, provokes the enemy, replaces the political struggle by physical struggle, etc. In all these phrases, there is nothing but political cowardice.

The militia, as the strong organization of the vanguard, is in fact the surest defense against adventures, against individual terrorism, against bloody spontaneous explosions.

The militia is at the same time the only serious way of reducing to a minimum the civil war that fascism imposes upon the proletariat. Let the workers, despite the absence of a "revolutionary situation", occassionally correct the "papa's son" patriots in their own way, and the recruitment of new fascist bands will become incomparably more difficult.

But here the strategists, tangled in their own reasoning, bring forward against us still more stupefying arguments. We quote textually:

> "If we reply to the revolver shots of the fascists with other revolver shots," writes **l'Humanité** of October 23 [1934], "we lose sight of the fact that fascism is the product of the capitalist regime and that in fighting against fascism it is the entire system which we face."

It is difficult to accumulate in a few lines greater confusion or more errors. It is impossible to defend oneself against the fascists because they are – "a product of the capitalist regime". That means, we have to renounce the whole struggle, for all contemporary social evils are "products of the capitalist system".

When the fascists kill a revolutionist, or burn down the building of a proletarian newspaper, the workers are to sigh philosophically: "Alas! Murders and arson are products of the capitalist system", and go home with easy consciences. Fatalist prostration is substituted for the militant theory of Marx, to the sole advantage of the class enemy. The ruin of the petty bourgeoisie is, of course, the product of capitalism. The growth of the fascist bands is, in turn, a product of the ruin of the petty bourgeoisie. But on the other hand, the increase in the misery and the revolt of the proletariat are also products of capitalism, and the militia, in its turn, is the product of the sharpening of the class struggle. Why, then, for the "Marxists" of **l'Humanité**, are the fascist bands the legitimate product of capitalism and the workers' militia the illegitimate product of – the Trotskyists? It is impossible to make head or tail of this.

"We have to deal with the whole system," we are told.

How? Over the heads of human beings? The fascists in the different countries began with their revolvers and ended by destroying the whole "system" of workers' organizations. How else to check the armed offensive of the enemy if not by an armed defense in order, in our turn, to go over to the offensive.

l'Humanité now admits defense in words, but only in the form of "mass self-defense". The militia is harmful because, you see, it divides the combat detachments from the masses. But why then are there independent armed detachments among the fascists who are not cut off from the reactionary masses but who, on the contrary, arouse the courage and embolden those masses by their well-organized attacks? Or perhaps the proletarian mass is inferior in combative quality to the declassed petty bourgeoisie?

Hopelessly tangled, **l'Humanité** finally begins to hesitate: it appears that mass self-defense requires the creation of special "self-defense groups". In place of the rejected militia, special groups or detachments are proposed. It would seem at first sight that there is a difference only in the name. Certainly, the name proposed by **l'Humanité** means nothing. One can speak of "mass self-defense" but it is impossible to speak of "self-defense groups" since the purpose of the groups is not to defend themselves but the workers' organizations. However, it is not, of course, a question of the name. The "self-defense groups", according to

l'Humanité, must renounce the use of arms in order not to fall into "putschism". These sages treat the working-class like an infant who must not be allowed to hold a razor in his hands. Razors, moreover, are the monopoly, as we know, of the *Camelots du Roi* [French monarchists grouped around Charles Maurras' newspaper, **Action Française**, which was violently anti-democratic], who are a legitimate "product of capitalism" and who, with the aid of razors, have overthrown the "system" of democracy. In any case, how are the "self-defense groups" going to defend themselves against the fascist revolvers? "Ideologically", of course. In other words: they can hide themselves. Not having what they require in their hands, they will have to seek "self-defense" in their feet. And the fascists will in the meanwhile sack the workers' organizations with impunity. But if the proletariat suffers a terrible defeat, it will at any rate not have been guilty of "putschism". This fraudulent chatter, parading under the banner of "Bolshevism", arouses only disgust and loathing.

During the "third period" of happy memory – when the strategists of **l'Humanité** were afflicted with barricade delirium, "conquered" the streets every day and stamped as "social fascist" everyone who did not share their extravagances – we predicted: "The moment these gentlemen burn the tips of their fingers, they will become the worst opportunists." That prediction has now been completely confirmed. At a time when within the Socialist Party the movement in favor of the militia is growing and strengthening, the leaders of the so-called Communist Party run for the hose to cool down the desire of the advanced workers to organize themselves in fighting columns. Could one imagine a more demoralizing or more damning work than this?

> In the ranks of the Socialist Party sometimes this objection is heard: "A militia must be formed but there is no need of shouting about it."

One can only congratulate comrades who wish to protect the

practical side of the business from inquisitive eyes and ears. But it would be much too naive to think that a militia could be created unseen and secretly within four walls. We need tens, and later hundreds, of thousands of fighters. They will come only if millions of men and women workers, and behind them the peasants, understand the necessity for the militia and create around the volunteers an atmosphere of ardent sympathy and active support. Conspiratorial care can and must envelop only the *technical* aspect of the matter. The political campaign must be openly developed, in meetings, factories, in the streets and on the public squares.

The fundamental cadres of the militia must be the factory workers grouped according to their place of work, known to each other and able to protect their combat detachments against the provocations of enemy agents far more easily and more surely than the most elevated bureaucrats. Conspirative general staffs without an open mobilization of the masses will at the moment of danger remain impotently suspended in midair. Every working-class organization has to plunge into the job. In this question, there can be no line of demarcation between the working-class parties and the trade unions. Hand in hand, they must mobilize the masses. The success of the people militia will then be fully assured.

> "But where are the workers going to get arms" object the sober "realists" – that is to say, frightened philistines – "the enemy has rifles, cannon, tanks, gas, and airplanes. The workers have a few hundred revolvers and pocket knives."

In this objection, everything is piled up to frighten the workers. On the one hand, our sages identify the arms of the fascists with the armament of the state. On the other hand, they turn towards the state and demand that it disarm the fascists. Remarkable logic! In fact, their position is false in both cases. In France, the fascists are still far from controlling the state. On February 6, they entered in armed conflict with the state police. that is why it is false to speak of cannon and tanks when it is a matter of the *immediate* armed struggle against the fascists. The fascists, of course, are richer than we. It is easier for them to buy arms. But the workers are more numerous, more determined, more devoted, when they are conscious of a firm revolutionary leadership.

In addition to other sources, the workers can arm themselves at the expense of the fascists by systematically disarming them.

This is now one of the most serious forms of the struggle against fascism. When workers' arsenals will begin to stock up at the expense of the fascist arms depots, the banks nd trusts will be more prudent in financing the armament of their murderous guards. It would even be possible in this case – but in this case only – that the alarmed authorities would really begin to prevent the arming of the fascists in order not to provide an additional sources of arms for the workers. We have known for a long time that only a revolutionary tactic engenders, as a by-product, "reforms" or concessions from the government.

But how to disarm the fascists? Naturally, it is impossible to do so with newspaper articles alone. Fighting squads must be created. An intelligence service must be established. Thousands of informers and friendly helpers will volunteer from all sides when they realize that the business has been seriously undertaken by us. It requires a will to proletarian action.

But the arms of the fascists are, of course, not the only source. In France, there are more than one million organized workers. Generally speaking, this number is small. But it is entirely sufficient to make a beginning in the organization of a workers' militia. If the parties and unions armed only a tenth of their members, that would already be a force of 100,000 men. there is no doubt whatever that the number of volunteers who would come forward on the morrow of a "united front" appeal for a workers' militia would far exceed that number. The contributions of the parties and unions, collections and voluntary subscriptions, would within a month or two make it possible to assure the arming of 100,000 to 200,000 working-class fighters. The fascist rabble would immediately sink its tail between its legs. The whole perspective of development would become incomparably more favorable.

To invoke the absence of arms or other objective reasons to explain why no attempt has been made up to now to create a militia, is to fool oneself and others. The principle obstacle – one can say the only obstacle – has its roots in the conservative and passive character of the leaders of the workers' organizations. The skeptics who are the leaders do not believe in the strength of the proletariat. They put their hope in all sorts of miracles from above instead of giving a revolutionary outlet to the energies pulsing below. The socialist workers must compel their leaders to pass over immediately to the creation of the workers' militia or else give way to younger, fresher forces.

A strike is inconceivable without propaganda and without agitation. It is also inconceivable without pickets who, when they can, use persuasion, but when obliged, use force. The strike is the most elementary form of the class struggle which always combines, in varying proportions, "ideological" methods with physical methods. The struggle against fascism is basically a political struggle which needs a militia just as the strike needs pickets. Basically, the picket is the embryo of the workers' militia. He who thinks of renouncing "physical" struggle must renounce all struggle, for the spirit does not live without flesh.

Following the splendid phrase of the great military theoretician Clausewitz, war is the continuation of politics by other means. This definition also fully applies to civil war. It is impermissable to oppose one to the other since it is impossible to check at will the political struggle when it transforms itself, by force of inner necessity, into a political struggle.

The duty of a revolutionary party is to foresee in time the

inescapability of the transformation of politics into open armed conflict, and with all its forces to prepare for that moment just as the ruling classes are preparing.

The militia detachments for defense against fascism are the first step on the road to the arming of the proletariat, not the last. Our slogan is:

"Arm the proletariat and the revolutionary peasants!"

The workers' militia must, in the final analysis, embrace all the toilers. To fulfill this program *completely* would be possible only in a workers' state into whose hands would pass all the means of production and, consequently, also all the means of destruction – i.e., all the arms and the factories which produce them.

However, it is impossible to arrive at a workers' state with empty hands. Only political invalids like Renaudel can speak of a peaceful, constitutional road to socialism. The constitutional road is cut by trenches held by the fascist bands. There are not a few trenches before us. The bourgeoisie will not hesitate to resort to a dozen coups d'etat, aided by the police and the army, to prevent proletariat from coming to power.

*[NOTE: Pierre Renaudel (1871–1935): Prior to WWI, socialist leader Jean Jaures' righthand man and editor of **l'Humanité**. During the war, a right-wing social patriot. In the 1930s, he and Marcel Deat led revisionist "neo-socialist" tendency. Voted down at the July 1933 convention, this tendency split from the Socialist Party. After the fascist riots of February 6, 1934, most of the "neos" joined the Radical Party, the main party of French capitalism.]*

A workers' socialist state can be created only by a victorious revolution.

Every revolution is prepared by the march of economic and political development, but it is always decided by open armed conflicts between hostile classes. A revolutionary victory can become possible only as a result of long political agitation, a lengthy period of education and organization of the masses.

But the armed conflict itself must likewise be prepared long in advance.

The advanced workers must know that they will have to fight and win a struggle to the death. They must reach out for arms, as a guarantee of their emancipation.

THE PERSPECTIVE IN THE UNITED STATES

From Some Questions on American Problems, **Fourth International**, October 1940

The backwardness of the United State working class is only a relative term.

In very many important respects, it is the most progressive working class of the world, technically and in its standard of living ...

The American workers are very combative – as we have seen during the strikes. They have had the most rebellious strikes in the world. What the American worker misses is a spirit of generalization, or analysis, of his class position in society as a whole. This lack of social thinking has its origin in the country's whole history ...

About fascism.

In all the countries where fascism became victorious, we had, before the growth of fascism and its victory, a wave of radicalism of the masses – of the workers and the poorer peasants and farmers, and of the petty bourgeois class. In Italy, after the war and before

1922, we had a revolutionary wave of tremendous dimensions; the state was paralyzed, the police did not exist, the trade unions could do anything they wanted – but there was not party capable of taking the power. As a reaction came fascism.

In Germany, the same. We had a revolutionary situation in 1918; the bourgeois class did not even ask to participate in the power. The social democrats paralyzed the revolution. Then the workers tried again in 1922–23–24. This was the time of the bankruptcy of the Communist Party – all of which we have gone into before. Then in 1929–30–31, the German workers began again a new revolutionary wave. There was a tremendous power in the Communists and in the trade unions, but then came the famous policy (on the part of the Stalinist movement) of social fascism, a policy invented to paralyze the working class. Only after these three tremendous waves did fascism become a big movement. There are no exceptions to this rule – fascism comes only when the working class shows complete incapacity to take into its own hands the fate of society.

In the United States you will have the same thing. Already, there are fascist elements, and they have, of course, the examples of Italy and germany. They will, therefore, work in a more rapid tempo. But you also have the examples of other countries. The next historic wave in the United States will be the wave of radicalism of the masses, not fascism. Of course, the war can hinder the radicalization for some time, but then it will give to the radicalization a more tremendous tempo and swing.

We must not identify war dictatorship – the dictatorship of the military machine, of the staff, of finance capital – with a fascist dictatorship. For the latter, there is first necessary a feeling of desperation of large masses of the people. When the revolutionary parties betray them, when the vanguard of workers shows it incapacity to lead the people to victory – then the farmers, the small business men, the unemployed, the soldiers, etc., become capable of supporting a fascist movement, but only then.

A military dictatorship is purely a bureaucratic institution, reinforced by the military machine and based upon the disorientation of the people and their submission to it. After some time their feelings can change and they can become rebellious against the dictatorship.

BUILD THE REVOLUTIONARY PARTY!

In every discussion of political topics the question arises:

Shall we succeed in creating a strong party for the moment when the crisis comes? Might not fascism anticipate us? Isn't a fascist stage of development inevitable?

The successes of fascism easily make people lose all perspective, lead them to forget the actual conditions which made the strengthening and the victory of fascism possible. Yet a clear understanding of these conditions is of especial importance to the workers of he United States. *We may set it down as a historical law: fascism was able to conquer only in those countries where the conservative labor parties prevented the proletariat from utilizing the revolutionary situation and seizing power.* In Germany two revolutionary situations were involved: 1918–1919 and 1923–1924. Even in 1929, a direct struggle for power on the part of the proletariat was still possible. In all these three cases, the social democracy and the Comintern [the Stalinists] criminally and viciously disrupted the conquest of power and thereby placed society in an impasse. Only under these conditions and in this situation did the stormy rise of fascism and its gaining of power prove possible.

* * *

In so far as the proletariat proves incapable, at a given stage, of conquering power, imperialism begins regulating economic life with its own methods; the fascist party which becomes the state power is the political mechanism. The productive forces are in irreconcilable contradiction not only with private property but also with national state boundaries. Imperialism is the very expression of this contradiction. Imperialist capitalism seeks to solve this contradiction through an extension of boundaries, seizure of new territories, and so on. The totalitarian state, subjecting all aspects of economic, political, and cultural life to finance capital, is the instrument for creating a supernationalist state, an imperialist empire, the rule over continents, the rule over the whole world.

All these traits of freedom we have analyzed, each one by itself and all of them in their totality, to the extent that they became manifest or came to the forefront.

Both theoretical analysis as well as the rich historical experience of the last quarter of a century have demonstrated with equal force that fascism is each time the final link of a specific political cycle composed of the following: the gravest crisis of capitalist society; the growth of the radicalization of the working class; the growth of sympathy toward the working class, and a yearning for change on the part of the rural and urban petty bourgeoisie; the extreme confusion of the big bourgeoisie; its cowardly and treacherous maneuvers aimed at avoiding the revolutionary climax; the exhaustion of the proletariat; growing confusion and indifference; the aggravation of the social crisis; the despair of the petty bourgeoisie, its yearning for change; the collective neurosis of the petty bourgeoisie, its readiness to believe in miracles, its readiness for violent measures; the growth of hostility towards the proletariat, which has deceived its expectations. These are the premises for a swift formation of a fascist party and its victory.

It is quite self-evident that the radicalization of the working class in the United States has passed through only its initial phases, almost exclusively, in the sphere of the trade union movement (the CIO). The prewar period, and then the war itself, may temporarily interrupt this process of radicalization, especially if a considerable number of workers are absorbed into war industry. But this interruption of the process of radicalization cannot be of a long duration. The second stage of radicalization will assume a more sharply expressive character. The problem of forming an independent labor party will be put on the order of the day. Our transitional demands will gain great popularity. On the other hand, the fascist, reactionary tendencies will withdraw to the background, assuming a defensive position, awaiting a more favorable moment. This is the nearest perspective. No occupation is more completely unworthy than that of speculating whether or not we shall succeed in creating a powerful revolutionary leader-party. Ahead lies a favorable perspective, providing all the justification for revolutionary activism. It is necessary to utilize the opportunities which are opening up and to build the revolutionary party.

FOOTNOTE BY MIA

A. This paragraph did not appear in the edition of the pamphlet used to digitise this text. However, it has appeared in other editions.

∗ ∗ ∗

LIST OF TITLES WITH ISBN NO.

ISBN	TITLE
9788194914129	1984
9789390575220	1984 & Animal Farm (2In1)
9789390575572	1984 & Animal Farm (2In1): The International Best-Selling Classics
9789390575848	35 Sonnets
9789390575329	A Clergyman's Daughter
9789390575923	A Study In Scarlet
9789390896097	A Tale Of Two Cities
9789390896837	Abide in Christ
9789390896202	Abraham Lincoln
9789390896912	Absolute Surrender
9789390896608	African American Classic Collection
9789390575305	Aldous Huxley: The Collected Works
9789390896141	An Autobiography of M. K. Gandhi
9789390575886	Animal Farm
9789390575619	Animal Farm & The Great Gatsby (2In1)
9789390575626	Animal Farm & We
9789390896158	Anna Karenina
9789390575534	Antic Hay
9789390896165	Antony & Cleopatra
9789390896172	As I Lay Dying
9789390896226	As You like it
9789390575671	At Your Command
9789390575350	Awakened Imagination
9789390575114	Be What You Wish
9789390896233	Believe In yourself
9789390896998	Best of Charles Darwin: The Origin of Species & Autobiography
9789390896684	Best Of Horror : Dracula And Frankenstein
9789390575503	Best Of Mark Twain (The Adventures of Tom Sawyer AND The Adventures of Huckleberry Finn)
9789390896769	Black History Collection
9789390575756	Brave New World, Animal Farm & 1984 (3in1)

ISBN	Title
9789390896240	Brother Karamzov
9789390575053	Bulleh Shah Poetry
9789390575725	Burmese Days
9789390896257	Bushido
9789390896066	Can't Hurt Me
9788194914112	Chanakya Neeti: With The Complete Sutras
9789390896042	Crime and Punishment
9789390575527	Crome Yellow
9789390575046	Down and Out in Paris and London
9789390896844	Dracula
9789390575442	Emersons Essays: The Complete First & Second Series (Self-Reliance & Other Essays)
9789390575749	Emma
9789390575817	Essential Tozer Collection - The Pursuit of God & The Purpose of Man
9789390896578	Fascism What It Is and How to Fight It
9789390575688	Feeling is the Secret
9789390575190	Five Lessons
9789390575954	Frankenstein
9789390575237	Franz Kafka: Collected Works
9789390575282	Franz Kafka: Short Stories
9789390575060	George Orwell Collected Works
9789390575077	George Orwell Essays
9789390575213	George Orwell Poems
9788194914150	Greatest Poetry Ever Written Vol 1
9788194914143	Greatest Poetry Ever Written Vol 1
9789390896301	Gulliver's Travel
9789390575961	Gunaho Ka Devta
9789390575893	H. P. Lovecraft Selected Stories Vol 1
9789390575978	H. P. Lovecraft Selected Stories Vol 2
9789390896059	Hamlet
9789390575022	His Last Bow: Some Reminiscences of Sherlock Holmes
9789390896134	History of Western Philosophy
9789390575121	Homage To Catalonia

ISBN	Title
9789390896219	How to develop self-confidence and Improve public Speaking
9789390896295	How to enjoy your life and your Job
9789390575633	How to own your own mind
9789390896318	How to read Human Nature
9789390896325	How to sell your way through the life
9789390896370	How to use the laws of mind
9789390896387	How to use the power of prayer
9789390896028	How to win friends & Influence People
9788194824176	How To Win Friends and Influence People
9789390896103	Humility The Beauty of Holiness
9789390896653	Imperialism the Highest Stage of Capitalism
9789390575084	In Our Time
9789390575169	In Our Time & Three Stories and Ten poems
9789390575145	James Allen: The Collected Works
9789390896189	Jesus Himself
9789390575480	Jo's Boys
9789390896394	Julius Caesar
9789390575404	Keep the Aspidistra Flying
9789390896400	Kidnapped
9789390896424	King Lear
9789390575824	Lady Susan
9789390896455	Law of Success
9789390896264	Lincoln The Unknown
9789390575565	Little Men
9789390575640	Little Women
9788194914174	Lost Horizon
9789390896462	Macbeth
9789390896929	Man Eaters of Kumaon
9789390896523	Man The Dwelling Place of God
9789390896349	Man The Dwelling Place of God
9789390575909	Mansfield Park
9788194914136	Manto Ki 25 Sarvshreshth Kahaniya
9789390896509	Marxism, Anarchism, Communism
9789390575664	Mathematical Principles of Natural Philosophy

9788194914198	Meditations
9789390575800	Mein Kampf
9789390575794	Memory How To Develop, Train, And Use It
9789390896486	Mind Power
9789390896585	Money
9789390575039	Mortal Coils
9789390575770	My Life and Work
9789390896035	Narrative of the Life of Frederick Douglass
9789390575152	Neville Goddard: The Collected Works
9789390575985	Northanger Abbey
9789390896530	Notes From Underground
9789390896547	Oliver Twist
9789390575459	On War
9789390575541	One, None and a Hundred Thousand
9789390896554	Othelo
9789390575435	Out Of This World
9789390575015	Persuasion
9789390575510	Prayer The Art Of Believing
9789390575091	Pride and Prejudice
9789390896561	Psychic Perception
9789390575381	Rabindranath Tagore - 5 Best Short Stories Vol 2
9789390575367	Rabindranath Tagore - Short Stories (Masters Collections Including The Childs Return)
9789390575374	Rabindranath Tagore 5 Best Short Stories Vol 1 (Including The Childs Return
9789390896622	Romeo & Juliet
9789390896127	Sanatana Dharma
9789390575596	Seedtime & Harvest
9789390896639	Selected Stories of Guy De Maupassant
9789390575206	Self-Reliance & Other Essays
9789390575176	Sense and Sensibility
9789390575299	Shyamchi Aai
9789390896738	Socialism Utopian and Scientific
9789390896646	Success Through a Positive Mental Attitude
9789390575428	The Adventures of Huckleberry Finn

ISBN	Title
9789390575183	The Adventures of Sherlock Holmes
9789390575343	The Adventures of Tom Sawyer
9789390896691	The Alchemy Of Happiness
9789390575862	The Art Of Public Speaking
9789390896288	The Autobiography Of Charles Darwin
9788194914181	The Best of Franz Kafka: The Metamorphosis & The Trial
9789390575008	The Call Of Cthulhu and Other Weird Tales
9789390575107	The Case-Book of Sherlock Holmes
9789390896110	The Castle Of Otranto
9789390896745	The Communist Manifesto
9789390575589	The Complete Fiction of H. P. Lovecraft
9789390575497	The Complete Works of Florence Scovel Shinn
9789390896820	The Conquest of Breard
9789390896813	The Diary of a Young Girl
9789390896332	The Diary of a Young Girl The Definitive Edition of the Worlds Most Famous Diary
9789390575701	The Great Gatsby, Animal Farm & 1984 (3In1)
9789390575312	The Greatest Works Of George Orwell (5 Books) Including 1984 & Non-Fiction
9789390575992	The Hound of Baskervilles
9789390896707	The Idiot
9789390896714	The Invisible Man
9789390575657	The Knowledge of the holy
9789390575558	The Law & the Promise
9789390896721	The Law Of Attraction
9789390896776	The Leader in you
9789390896363	The Life of Christ
9789390896196	The Man-Eating Leopard of Rudraprayag
9789390896783	The Master Key to Riches
9789390575268	The Memoirs Of Sherlock Holmes
9789390896479	The Midsummer Night's Dream
9789390575466	The Mill On The Floss
9789390896790	The Miracles of your mind
9789390896660	The Mutual Aid A Factor in Evolution
9789390896448	The Origin of Species

ISBN	Title
9789390896905	The Peter Kropotkin Anthology The Conquest of Bread & Mutual Aid A Factor of Evolution
9789390896806	The Picture of Dorian Gray
9789390896271	The Picture of Dorian Gray
9789390575275	The Power Of Awareness
9789390896356	The Power of Concentration
9788194824169	The Power of Positive Thinking
9789390575411	The Power of the Spoken Word
9788194914105	The Power Of Your Subconscious Mind
9789390896899	The Power of Your Subconscious Mind
9789390896417	The Principles of Communism
9789390575787	The Psychology Of Mans Possible Evolution
9789390896615	The Psychology of Salesmanship
9789390575732	The Pursuit of God
9789390575398	The Pursuit of Happiness
9789390896851	The Quick and Easy Way to effective Speaking
9789390575947	The Return Of Sherlock Holmes
9789390575138	The Road To Wigan Pier
9789390896981	The Root of the Righteous
9789390575855	The Science Of Being Well
9788194914167	The Science Of Getting Rich, The Science Of Being Great & The Science Of Being Well (3In1)
9789390896011	The Screwtape Letters
9789390896073	The Screwtape Letters
9789390575336	The Secret Door to Success
9789390575695	The Secret Of Imagining
9789390896868	The Secret Of Success
9789390896431	The Seven Last Words
9789390575930	The Sign of the Four
9789390896004	The Sonnets
9789390896516	The Souls of Black Folk
9789390896875	The Sound and The Fury
9789390575244	The State and Revolution
9789390896882	The Story of My Life
9789390896936	The Story Of Oriental Philosophy

ISBN	Title
9789390896752	The Strange Case of Dr. Jekyll and Mr. Hyde
9789390896943	The Tempest
9789390575916	The Valley Of Fear
9789390575879	The Wind in the willows
9789390896080	The Wind in the willows
9789390575763	Their eyes were watching gofd
9789390575831	Three Stories
9789390896950	Twelfth Night
9789390896592	Twelve Years a Slave
9789390896677	Up from Slavery
9789390896974	Value Price and Profit
9789390896967	Wake Up and Live
9789390896493	With Christ in the School of Prayer
9789390575602	Your Faith is Your Fortune
9789390575473	Your Infinite Power To Be Rich
9789390575251	Your Word is Your Wand
9789390575718	Youth
9789391316099	A Christmas Carol
9789391316105	A Doll's House
9789391316501	A Passage to India
9789391316709	A Portrait of the Artist as a Young Man
9789391316112	A Tale of Two Cities
9789391316747	A Tear and a Smile
9789391316167	Agnes Gray
9789391316174	Alice's Adventures in Wonderland
9789391316136	Anandamath
9789391316181	Anne Of Green Gables
9789391316754	Anthem
9789391316198	Around The World in 80 Days
9789391316013	As A Man Thinketh
9789391316242	Autobiography of a Yogi
9789391316266	Beyond Good and Evil
9789391316761	Bleak House
9789391316778	Chitra, a Play in One Act
9789391316310	David Copperfield

9789391316075	Demian
9789391316785	Dubliners
9789391316051	Favourite Tales from the Arabian Nights
9789391316235	Gitanjali
9789391316068	Gravity
9789391316150	Great Speeches of Abraham Lincoln
9789391316662	Guerilla Warfare
9789391316839	Kim
9789391316822	Mother
9789391316211	My Childhood
9789391316846	Nationalism
9789391316327	Oliver Twist
9789391316853	Pygmalion
9789391316334	Relativity: The Special and the General Theory
9789391316389	Scientific Healing Affirmation
9789391316341	Sons and Lovers
9789391316587	Tales from India
9789391316372	Tess of The D'Urbervilles
9789391316396	The Awakening and Selected Stories
9789391316402	The Bhagvad Gita
9789391316303	The Book of Enoch
9789391316228	The Canterville Ghost
9789391316907	The Dynamic Laws of Prosperity
9789391316006	The Great Gatsby
9789391316860	The Hungry Stones and Other Stories
9789391316433	The Idiot
9789391316440	The Importance of Being Earnest
9789391316297	The Light of Asia
9789391316914	The Madman His Parables and Poems
9789391316457	The Odyssey
9789391316921	The Picture of Dorian Gray
9789391316464	The Prince
9789391316938	The Prophet
9789391316945	The Republic
9789391316518	The Scarlet Letter

ISBN	Title
9789391316143	The Seven Laws of Teaching
9789391316525	The Story of My Experiments with Truth
9789391316532	The Tales of the Mother Goose
9789391316549	The Thirty Nine Steps
9789391316594	The Time Machine
9789391316600	The Turn of the Screw
9789391316983	The Upanishads
9789391316617	The Yellow Wallpaper
9789391316426	The Yoga Sutras of Patanjali
9789391316990	Ulysses
9789391316624	Utopia
9789391316679	Vanity Fair
9789391316020	What Is To Be Done
9789391316686	Within A Budding Grove
9789391316693	Women in Love

www.ingramcontent.com/pod-product-compliance
Ingram Content Group UK Ltd.
Pitfield, Milton Keynes, MK11 3LW, UK
UKHW040635080725
6782UKWH00002B/7